WorkBook

for

Building a Life Worth Living

Mezil Publishing

Disclaimer

This workbook is an unofficial companion to the original book. It is not endorsed, sponsored, or associated with the original author, or publisher of the original book. All views and opinions expressed in this workbook are those of the author and do not necessarily reflect the views and opinions of the author or publisher of the original book

This book belongs to

Introduction

Having immersed myself in Linehan's original book, I was captivated by the depth of her understanding and her unwavering belief that every individual has the potential to lead a life filled with purpose and contentment.

The book explores a wide range of topics, from cultivating mindfulness and emotion regulation to navigating relationships and creating a meaningful life vision. Linehan's compassionate approach and evidence-based techniques provide a roadmap for healing and personal growth, making "Building a Life Worth Living" an indispensable guide for anyone yearning for positive change.

However, as I delved deeper into the material, I realized that an unofficial workbook could enhance the reader's engagement and facilitate a more profound exploration of Linehan's teachings. This workbook aims to provide readers with an interactive experience, helping them internalize and apply the principles presented in the main book to their own lives.

The workbook comprises a series of thought-provoking exercises, reflection prompts, and practical activities designed to encourage self-reflection, enhance understanding, and foster personal transformation.

Each chapter aligns with the corresponding themes discussed in "Building a Life Worth Living," enabling readers to delve further into the concepts, internalize the knowledge, and embark on their own journey towards a life worth living.

Through the workbook, readers will have the opportunity to delve into their emotions, examine their patterns of thinking and behaving, and develop a personalized toolkit for emotional well-being and personal growth. The exercises and activities within this workbook are designed to promote self-awareness, cultivate resilience, and empower readers to make meaningful changes in their lives.

Creating this workbook was a labor of love, inspired by the belief that every person deserves the chance to live a life filled with purpose, joy, and genuine connection. It is my hope that this accompanying resource will serve as a trusted companion, offering guidance, support, and a roadmap towards building a life worth living.

In the pages that follow, I invite you to embark on a transformative journey—a journey of self-discovery, healing, and personal growth. Together, let us explore the principles and practices outlined in "Building a Life Worth Living" and create a foundation for lasting change.

.

What are your core values and beliefs that give your life meaning and purpose?

_____

_____

_____

_____

_____

_____

_____

_____

_____

_____

_____

_____

How can you align your daily actions and decisions with these values to create a sense of fulfilment and joy?

_____

_____

_____

_____

_____

_____

_____

_____

_____

_____

_____

_____

How can you practice self-compassion and treat yourself with kindness during difficult times?

_____

_____

_____

_____

_____

_____

_____

_____

_____

_____

_____

_____

What strategies can you employ to challenge self-critical thoughts and develop a more nurturing and supportive inner dialogue?

_____

_____

_____

_____

_____

_____

_____

_____

_____

_____

_____

Who are the people in your life that you can rely on for support during challenging moments?

_____

_____

_____

_____

_____

_____

_____

_____

_____

_____

_____

_____

_____

How can you communicate your needs to them and ask for assistance when necessary?

_____

_____

_____

_____

_____

_____

_____

_____

_____

_____

_____

_____

_____

How can you actively nurture and strengthen these relationships?

_____

_____

_____

_____

_____

_____

_____

_____

_____

_____

_____

_____

What are the specific situations, events, or thoughts that tend to trigger feelings of depression and suicidal thoughts for you?

_____

_____

_____

_____

_____

_____

_____

_____

_____

_____

_____

_____

How can you become more aware of these triggers and develop strategies to manage them effectively?

_____

_____

_____

_____

_____

_____

_____

_____

_____

_____

_____

_____

What healthy coping mechanisms have you found helpful in managing depressive episodes?

_____

_____

_____

_____

_____

_____

_____

_____

_____

_____

_____

_____

How can you expand your repertoire of coping strategies to include activities such as exercise, mindfulness, journaling, or creative outlets?

_____

_____

_____

_____

_____

_____

_____

_____

_____

_____

_____

_____

_____

What negative or self-defeating thoughts tend to arise when you are feeling depressed?

_____

_____

_____

_____

_____

_____

_____

_____

_____

_____

_____

How can you identify and challenge these distorted thoughts with more balanced and realistic thinking patterns?

_____

_____

_____

_____

_____

_____

_____

_____

_____

_____

_____

_____

During times of crisis, having a safety plan in place is crucial. What are some steps you can take to ensure your safety and well-being in those moments?

_____

_____

_____

_____

_____

_____

_____

_____

_____

_____

_____

_____

Who can you reach out to for immediate support? Are there helplines or crisis resources you can access?

_____

_____

_____

_____

_____

_____

_____

_____

_____

_____

_____

_____

What activities or hobbies bring you a sense of joy and purpose?

_____

_____

_____

_____

_____

_____

_____

_____

_____

_____

_____

_____

_____

How can you incorporate more of these meaningful activities into your daily life, even when you're feeling down?

_____

_____

_____

_____

_____

_____

_____

_____

_____

_____

_____

Reflecting on your values and beliefs, how can you align your daily actions with what truly matters to you?

_____

_____

_____

_____

_____

_____

_____

_____

_____

_____

_____

_____

_____

How can you overcome these barriers and take the necessary steps to access the support you need?

_____

_____

_____

_____

_____

_____

_____

_____

_____

_____

_____

_____

How can you cultivate resilience and bounce back from challenging situations

_____

_____

_____

_____

_____

_____

_____

_____

_____

_____

_____

_____

_____

Are there specific skills or practices you can develop to help you navigate difficulties more effectively?

_____

_____

_____

_____

_____

_____

_____

_____

_____

_____

_____

_____

_____

What activities or experiences bring you a deep sense of fulfillment and joy?

_____

_____

_____

_____

_____

_____

_____

_____

_____

_____

_____

_____

_____

What long-term goals or aspirations do you have that align with your sense of purpose?

_____

_____

_____

_____

_____

_____

_____

_____

_____

_____

_____

_____

_____

_____

How can you incorporate more meaning and purpose into your personal and professional life?

_____

_____

_____

_____

_____

_____

_____

_____

_____

_____

_____

_____

_____

How can you incorporate more mindfulness and self-reflection into your life to enhance your emotional and mental well-being?

_____

_____

_____

_____

_____

_____

_____

_____

_____

_____

_____

_____

_____

Reflecting on past challenges or setbacks, what lessons did you learn from those experiences?

_____

_____

_____

_____

_____

_____

_____

_____

_____

_____

_____

_____

_____

How can you cultivate resilience in the face of adversity?

_____

_____

_____

_____

_____

_____

_____

_____

_____

_____

_____

_____

_____

Are there any limiting beliefs or self-doubts that hinder your personal growth? How can you challenge and overcome them?

_____

_____

_____

_____

_____

_____

_____

_____

_____

_____

_____

_____

What opportunities for personal and professional growth excite and motivate you?

_____

_____

_____

_____

_____

_____

_____

_____

_____

_____

_____

_____

_____

How can you establish a healthy work-life balance that allows you to thrive in both areas?

_____

_____

_____

_____

_____

_____

_____

_____

_____

_____

_____

_____

Are there any boundaries or routines you can set to prevent work from overwhelming other aspects of your life?

_____

_____

_____

_____

_____

_____

_____

_____

_____

_____

_____

_____

How can you cultivate a sense of fulfilment
and purpose within your professional life?

_____

_____

_____

_____

_____

_____

_____

_____

_____

_____

_____

_____

_____

How can you incorporate gratitude practices into your daily life to foster a positive mindset?

_____

_____

_____

_____

_____

_____

_____

_____

_____

_____

_____

_____

Are there any mindfulness techniques or meditation practices that resonate with you? How can you incorporate them into your routine?

_____

_____

_____

_____

_____

_____

_____

_____

_____

_____

_____

_____

How can you become more aware of and savor the present moment, rather than constantly focusing on the future or dwelling on the past?

_____

_____

_____

_____

_____

_____

_____

_____

_____

_____

_____

_____

_____

How can you reframe challenges and setbacks as opportunities for growth and learning?

_____

_____

_____

_____

_____

_____

_____

_____

_____

_____

_____

_____

_____

Made in the USA
Las Vegas, NV
07 December 2024

13542624R00024